Edward Delves

A Brief Description of the Hamlet of Heighham, Norwich

It's Ancient And Modern History, Churches, Chapels, Population, etc

Edward Delves

A Brief Description of the Hamlet of Heighham, Norwich
It's Ancient And Modern History, Churches, Chapels, Population, etc

ISBN/EAN: 9783744725491

Printed in Europe, USA, Canada, Australia, Japan

Cover: Foto ©ninafisch / pixelio.de

More available books at **www.hansebooks.com**

A BRIEF DESCRIPTION

OF THE

HAMLET OF HEIGHAM,

NORWICH:

ITS

ANCIENT AND MODERN HISTORY,

CHURCHES, CHAPELS, POPULATION, ETC.

———————

COMPILED FROM VARIOUS SOURCES BY

EDWARD DELVES.

———————

NORWICH:
PRINTED AT THE "NORFOLK NEWS" OFFICE, ST. ANDREW'S,
1879.

TO

J. J. WINTER, Esq.

(Who for many years has resided in Heigham, and, with his Father before
him, has always evinced the greatest interest in all matters
connected with the welfare of the Parish),

THIS   LITTLE   WORK

IS

𝔐𝔬𝔰𝔱 𝔕𝔢𝔰𝔭𝔢𝔠𝔱𝔣𝔲𝔩𝔩𝔶 𝔇𝔢𝔡𝔦𝔠𝔞𝔱𝔢𝔡

BY HIS HUMBLE SERVANT,

THE COMPILER.

Gladstone Street, North Heigham,
October, 1879.

CONTENTS.

THE

HAMLET OF HEIGHAM.

ANCIENT HISTORY.

N pre-historic times, Norfolk was not so extensive a tract of country as it now is, as the sea formerly covered thousands of acres of land which are now either grazing marshes or under cultivation. All the marsh lands lying between Yarmouth and Norwich, as well as the low-lying parts of the latter city itself, including some portions of Heigham, were then under water. In process of time, some important geological changes occurred ; a sandbank was formed across the mouth of the Yare, on which Yarmouth grew, and the waters, thus held back, gradually fell to their present level.

HEHAM, EEHAM, or, as it is now called, HEIGHAM, was formerly a small village on the banks of the River Wensum, whence its name, Ea-ham or He-ham signifying "The Village at the Water."* It is now included in the county of the

---

* This derivation from Blomefield differs somewhat from that given by the Rev. G. Munford in his "Local Names in Norfolk." Mr. Munford takes the prefix from the Anglo-Saxon *Heag* or *heah*, "high ;" and the final syllable from the Anglo-Saxon *Ham*, signifying a "home" or "village."

city of Norwich ; but in ancient times it formed a part of
the Hundred of Humbleyard, Norfolk. The "town" was
given by Wulfricus, a Saxon, to the Abbey of St. Benet's-
at-Holme, as appears from Domesday Book, at the foundation
of that abbey in 1020 by King Canute.* It was estimated
at three carucates,† two of which were demesnes, and the
other was in the hands of the tenants. The whole in the
time of Edward the Confessor was valued at £4, and in the
Conqueror's time at £5 yearly. William, the first Abbot of
St. Benet's, granted to Thomas, the son of Thurburn the
priest, the town of Heham in fee-farm for life ; and William,
the second abbot, granted it to Richard Bassett on the same
tenure, at £10 a-year, and agreed to receive him into the
fraternity of the convent, and annually to keep his obit.

In the time of Henry II. a fine was levied of this manor,
when it was confirmed to the Abbot by William de Neovillâ,
or Neville, and Henry his brother ; and the King gave special
orders that the abbot should not lose that part of his land
enclosed within the new ditch which the burgesses of Norwich
had made without the city, after the death of Henry I. This
grant included all Nether or Lower Heigham, which was
always reckoned as a part of the suburbs of Norwich, and
was made the boundary of the liberties of the city on that
side.‡

In the time of Henry III. the abbot had confirmed to him
view of frank-pledge,§ assize of bread and ale, a common
gallows, and other liberties, provided that the King's bailiff

---

* This celebrated abbey was situate at Horning, a small village about nine
miles from Norwich. A part of the foundation of the walls, the remains of the
principal gateway, and other ruins, still exist.

† A "carucate" means as much land as one team could plough in a year, and
has been variously estimated by different authorities at from 100 to 140 acres.

‡ Blomefield's " History of Norwich," p. 849.

§ " Frank-pledge" means a pledge or surety for freemen. Every person, free
born (knights and their eldest sons, and those of the religious order excepted),
on attaining the age of twelve years, was in ancient times obliged to find surety

of Humbleyard Hundred was permitted to be present in court, and that he was paid a yearly stipend of two shillings. The manor was then held as part of the abbot's barony of Tunstead.

In 1227, the abbot granted to Peter and Nicholas Chese twenty-four acres of land and half a water-mill in Heigham, with common of pasture for two hundred sheep; and in 1242 he conveyed to Robert Hauteyn common of fishery in the waters and rivers of Heham and Hellesdon, from the head of the mill-dam in Heham, on both sides of the river, to Kelbe's acre; and William le Boteler released to Nicholas, Abbot of St. Benet's, all his right of commonage in King's Holme and Unkelbeve meadow, and elsewhere in this town. These mills were called Chese's, Bumpstede's, Appleyard's, or Westwick Mills, and stood near Heigham Gates. There were two mills under one roof, one held of the abbot and the other of the prior. The earliest reference to these mills, according to Blomefield, is in the time of Edward the Confessor, when, it appears from Domesday Book, Bishop Egelmar or Almar, brother to Stigand, the Archbishop of Canterbury, held by patrimony the Church of St. Simon and Jude. To this church belonged three parts of a mill, half an acre of meadow, and one mansion; and in the opinion of our great historian, this mill, of which the burgesses of Norwich held the fourth part, was Westwick Mill. Bishop Herbert de Lozinga, it also appears, afterwards granted to the monks the mill, land, and meadow which anciently belonged to the bishopric, and which stood near where Heigham Gates were subsequently built.*

---

for fidelity to the king, whence it became customary for a certain number of neighbors to become bond for one another. This was called "Frank-pledge," and ten households commonly constituted a "decennary" or "tithing." The duty of inspecting a decennary or tithing was called a "View of Frank-pledge."

* Blomefield's "History of Norwich," p. 9, and Notes D and E.

In 1393 it was agreed and acknowledged by the city that the abbot's tenants and the parishioners of Heigham were not to be summoned or distrained by the bailiffs of Norwich in any case.

In 1430, the New Mills in Lower Westwick Street were erected, and proved a bone of contention between the Abbot of Holme and the worthy burgesses of Norwich for many years after. In 1440, the abbot, as lord of the manor and court of Heigham, and holder of two water-mills and 160 acres of land, proceeded against the city for erecting the New Mills upon the river, whereby he contended the citizens had prevented his boats having free passage to and from his Abbey of Holme. He also alleged that the new buildings, by stopping the current, had caused the water to overflow the banks of the stream, and so greatly damaged his lands. In answer to these charges, it was proved on behalf of the city that there had been four ancient mills standing across the stream since the Conqueror's time. Two of these mills stood outside the boundary of the city, and were afterwards known as Bumpstede's or Appleyard's; while the other two were within the city, and were called Calke Mills. The citizens averred that it was the abbot's mills which stopped the water, and so caused more damage than the New Mills. The abbot, however, contended that the stream used to be open, and that the old mills had stood across loop streams; but the city authorities produced evidence to show that from time immemorial, whenever boatmen went up the stream towards Taverham, they were obliged to land at old Calke Mills and Hellesdon Mills, and pull their boats across to the higher water. The matter was ultimately decided against the city, which had to pay damages to the abbot. This excited great wrath in Norwich against that dignitary; and the people riotously assembled, and took away the common seal from the Guildhall, so that the award of the commissioner to whom the matter was referred, and who decided the case, could not be ratified.*

In 1403, Norwich was granted a new charter by King Henry IV., which enacted that "the city, and all the land within the city, and the liberty of the same, with the suburbs, and their hamlets and their bounds, and all the land round the liberty thereof (certain portions only excepted), shall be and are hereby separated from the county of Norfolk, . . . and are hereby made a county of and by themselves, which shall be for ever called the County of the City of Norwich."

In 1549, Thomas Holl farmed the manor of the bishopric at £16 16s. 3d. per annum, and had for his fee as bailiff of it £4 per annum, and £4 16s. for six coombs of corn to be delivered at the Palace for the Bishop's use. The lease of the manor and estate was afterwards purchased and held for many years by the Seaman family.

In the time of Henry VIII., the Bishop of Norwich, as Abbot of St. Benet's-at-Holme, was possessed of all the spiritualities and temporalities of that abbey. Shortly before the dissolution of the other monasteries by King Henry, the revenues of this famed abbey, which included the manor, faldcourse, fishery, and advowson of the rectory of Heigham, were transferred by a private Act of Parliament to Bishop Rugg or Reppes, who was formerly Abbot of St. Benet's, in exchange with the Crown for all the ancient estates and revenues of the bishopric. The abbey in consequence escaped a formal dissolution, and has ever since remained annexed to the see of Norwich. It was a mitred abbey, for which reason its abbots always sat in Parliament; and by right of this exchange the Bishop of Norwich, the only mitred abbot now remaining in England, sits in the House of Lords. The

---

* Blomefield's "History of Norwich," p. 106-8.

last rector of Heigham presented by Holme Abbey was William Paye, A.M., in 1526; and in 1555, the Bishop, as Abbot of Holme, exercised his right by the appointment of Sir William Ascew or Askoe as rector.

In 1536, the Bishop of Norwich, as Abbot of St. Benet's, leased out all his water-mills in Heigham, with all the houses belonging thereto, "and a meadow between the mill-dam and the water descending from Scalby, and the great meadow, and the meadow surrounded with water coming from the said mills, lying on the east part thereof, and all the right of fishing from and against St. Laurence's Acre on the west part of the mill, unto and against the creek of water between Heigham Common and the great meadow on the east part of the same."[*]

In 1644, during the troublous times of the Civil War, Thomas Stokes, A.M., Rector of Heigham, was ejected out of this and Carleton Rode Rectory by the Earl of Manchester, a noted leader of the Parliamentary forces, for refusing to contribute in aid of the Rebellion. "After many intruders," says Blomefield, "Bishop Hall in 1652 instituted his friend, John Whitefoot, sen., into the rectory."

The rectory was valued in the King's Books, by the name of "Higham-by-Norwich," at £6 13s. 4d. At Norwich Domesday valuation there was neither house nor glebe, and it was valued at eight marks. The church, the principal portion of which is believed to have been erected early in the fifteenth century, is dedicated to St. Bartholomew. Blomefield says it formerly had a guild kept in it in honor of that saint and of the Blessed Virgin. The church is called in many wills "Staunford St. Bartilmew-next-Norwich;" while the "town" or parish is sometimes mentioned by the name of "Heham" or "Staunford." The church was a small

---

[*] Blomefield's "History of Norwich," p. 849-50.

structure in the Perpendicular style, with a nave, south aisle, vestry, north porch, and a square tower in which were three bells.* The entire length of the edifice, which was capable of seating barely 200 persons, was 26 yards; the breadth, including the aisle, being 11 yards. The fabric underwent considerable repairs at various periods, particularly during the last fifty years, as is apparent from the numerous entries in the churchwardens' accounts relating thereto. Until about forty years ago, adjoining the porch was a stable, in which a former minister, who lived at some distance from the church, used to put up his horse during divine service.

MODERN HISTORY.

Modern Heigham, which forms the largest suburb of the city of Norwich, and is pleasantly situated on the western side of that city, presents a strange contrast to the Heigham our forefathers knew. A few straggling houses, a small church, and an insignificant village scarcely a mile from the city gates, from which the parish was separated by frowning fortifications and a deep ditch, were all that it could boast of centuries ago. When "good Queen Bess," during her brief sojourn at Norwich in the year 1578, passed out of St. Benedict's Gates, through Heigham, on her way to hunt at Costessey Park, there was scarcely a house to be seen; and in later times, when the worthy citizens, on pleasure bent, wended their way to Heigham Water Frolic, an annual "institution" here for many years, they passed through a district surrounded on either side by green fields or waste lands. Even in the latter part of the 17th century

---

* One of these bells, which had an extensive crack in it, and a large piece several pounds in weight broken off, thereby rendering it useless, was taken down in 1837, re-cast by Mr. Hurry, and hung over the Episcopal Chapel in Union Place.—*Heigham Churchwardens' Books*, 1837.

the number of families resident in Heigham scarcely exceeded
a hundred ; while in 1752 there were only 653 inhabitants,
and the parish contained but 164 houses, a number exceeded
by those in course of erection in North Heigham alone in
the past year (1878).   In 1786, the population had risen to
923 ; but from that time up to the year 1801 there was a
decrease, the numbers returned for the latter year being 854.
This was probably owing to the fact that the figures for 1801
did not include those persons serving in the army, navy, or
militia ; and as England was at that time unhappily engaged
in a disastrous war, this made a perceptible difference in the
numbers returned, even for such a small place as Heigham,
where doubtless many of the young men volunteered for
service.   Norwich was always reckoned a famous recruiting
ground, and is said to have furnished upwards of 4000
recruits within three or four years' time for the war referred
to, which happily terminated in 1802, only, however, to
break out afresh a short time later, and make its influence
felt when the census was taken in 1811.

A comparison of the figures in the census returns taken
at various decades shows how Norwich must have altered its
appearance within the present century, when the exigencies
of modern times necessitated the extension of the city beyond
the walls.   As is well known, Norwich, with the exception
of those small portions protected by the river, was formerly
surrounded by a strong embattled wall, flanked with forty
towers.   These walls were commenced in 1294, and finished
in 1320 ; and, in order to allow of the egress and ingress of
the citizens, gates were made at various points, at which
soldiers were placed, and a general watch and ward kept at
night.   Heigham Gate was situated at the bottom of what
is now called Barn Road.   It was a postern only, capable
of admitting small carts with low loads to pass through.

According to Blomefield, it was anciently called "*Porta Inferna*, or Hell Gate, from its low situation, and the odd appearance that the street leading to it hath to any one that looks down it from Charing Cross ; being a prodigious chasm and declivity, like the entrance of the ancient poet's hell." It is not known when this gate was taken down or fell to ruins ; but there are portions of the walls still remaining. The other gates leading into Heigham were called St. Benedict's or Westwick Gates and St. Giles' Gates, and at short distances therefrom, without the city walls, lazar-houses formerly existed, which were used for the reception and isolation of persons afflicted with leprosy. An extensive ditch ran along the outside of the walls from one gate to another; and from the frequent reference there is to the various ditches being scoured and cleansed, one can imagine they proved the receptacle for all kinds of filth and refuse. In former times, whatever other burdens the citizens labored under, they had no costly drainage scheme to pay for. At seasons of heavy rainfall, the water rushed down the slope from St. Giles' in torrents, finding its way across St. Benedict's Street into the ditch along Barn Road, and thence somehow into the river at the back of the New Mills. The ditches were filled up at various periods, those on Barn Road and Rising Sun Road within the memory of persons living. In the churchwardens' books for Heigham in 1817-18 we find an entry which probably relates to the partial filling-up of one of the ditches :—"Coulder for the ditch, £3 1s. 7½d."

THE EPISCOPAL CHAPEL, UNION PLACE.

Early in the present century, the tide of migration from the city to the suburbs set in, and Heigham began to be built over rapidly. The population rose from 842 in 1811, to 1503 in 1821, when there were 362 houses in the parish.

In 1831, the number of souls had increased to 5396 ; and it was felt that something should be done in order to provide for the spiritual wants of those resident in that portion of the district situated furthest from the parish church, where many new houses had been erected.   Moreover, the church was capable of accommodating only a very limited number of persons, and was situated in an out-of-the-way corner of the parish.   Accordingly, in 1837, the Rev. W. Robbins, M.A., then rector, purchased a large building in Union Place as a Chapel-of-Ease.   It had for twelve or thirteen years previously been used by the Baptist denomination, and was called Rehoboth Chapel, being situated in the centre of a district becoming more thickly populated every year.   The building was opened by license of the Bishop on the 10th of September, 1837, according to the rites of the Church of England; and on January 16th, 1839, the chapel, which was called the Episcopal Chapel, and was capable of seating about 500 persons, was consecrated by Bishop Stanley.   The building continued in use as a place in which to hold divine service for nearly twenty-five years ; but at a vestry meeting in September, 1861, shortly after the erection of the new church in Essex Street, it was decided to convert it into a Day and Sunday School for South Heigham.

THE BRITISH SCHOOLS, SAYER'S BUILDINGS.

Notwithstanding the rapid increase which took place in the population of Heigham early in the present century, there was scarcely any provision for the education of the youthful portion of its inhabitants until about thirty-five years ago.   There were at that time at least 6000 persons resident in the parish, and the only public schools open to the children of the poor were held in small rooms capable of affording accommodation to but a very limited number.

In 1845, however, through the liberality of Mr. (afterwards Sir) Morton Peto, who subsequently represented Norwich in Parliament, a school for girls, boys, and infants was erected in the locality now called Sayer's Buildings, near Heigham Street. It was vested in trustees, and was conducted under the British and Foreign School Society's system, viz., that of allowing the Bible to be read without note or comment. The good work was carried on for many years under efficient managers; but shortly after the introduction of the School Board system into Norwich, it was determined to discontinue the day schools. The building is, however, still used, as from the outset, for the purposes of a Sunday School.

THE NATIONAL SCHOOLS.

Profiting from the example set them by their Dissenting brethren, a number of influential inhabitants of Heigham, connected with the Church of England, set to work a year or two later to provide school accommodation for the parish in accordance with the views advocated by the National Society for Promoting the Education of the Poor in the Principles of the Established Church; and a movement was started in 1847 for the erection of suitable buildings on the Dereham Road, amongst its most active supporters being the rector, the Rev. W. Robbins, J. Winter, Esq., T. Steward, Esq., R. Blake-Humfrey, Esq., and other landowners and residents in the hamlet. A bazaar was held on Mr. Winter's grounds in aid of the project, and a considerable sum realised thereby. The erection of the schools, which cost about £1000, was commenced in the summer of 1848, the builders being Messrs. Curtis and Balls. The building is a neat and substantial structure in the Tudor style of architecture, and affords accommodation for over 200 scholars, although not usually attended by so large a number. The opening of the schools was celebrated in July, 1849, in the presence of a numerous company of ladies and gentlemen, including the Bishop of the Diocese (Dr. Stanley), and the Mayor of Norwich (S. Bignold, Esq.) The present Sheriff of Norwich (D. Steward, Esq.), and J. J. Winter, Esq., were the first honorary secretaries for these schools, and remained so for many years, taking great interest in them.

THE CITY OF NORWICH WATERWORKS.

The City of Norwich Waterworks are in Heigham, and supply the city and its suburbs with pure filtered water from the River Wensum. Formerly, from an early period, the city was served with water from works on the river belonging to the Corporation, and situate at the New Mills, which were let on lease to various parties. In the year 1710, these mills and waterworks were rebuilt ; but the general supply of water to the citizens was not attempted until a later period, and even then it was deficient both in quantity and quality. Many of the houses in the poorer parts of the city were unprovided with either pump or pipe, and the water was taken from a point of the river subject to the contamination of the refuse from the district adjoining Heigham Street on the one side, and a portion of St. Martin's on the other, below some foul and offensive sewers, felmongers' yards, bathing-places, and the like. The citizens were naturally dissatisfied with this state of things ; and in 1849, when Norwich, like other places in the kingdom, suffered to a small extent from a visitation of cholera, public attention was drawn to the subject. The formation of a new company was suggested, with the object of obtaining a constant supply of water from a point higher up the river, near Heigham Common. The requisite number of shares were speedily taken up, and the company was incorporated by Act of Parliament, 13th and

14th Vic., with a capital of £60,000 in £10 shares. The works were commenced early in 1851, and late in the same year a good supply of water was first forced from the works at Heigham into a distributing reservoir at Lakenham, at a height of 134 feet above the level of the river at Carrow Bridge. From Lakenham the water, which is reckoned as exceedingly pure, flows by gravitation to all parts of the city and its suburbs. The contractors for the works were Messrs. Lucas Bros., the engineer being Mr. Lynde. Mr. Ayris, C.E., of Heigham Grove, is the present engineer.

THE CEMETERY.

One of the greatest improvements effected in Norwich, about the middle of the present century, was the closing of all the churchyards for burial purposes. The tide of public opinion had set in strongly against the practice of interring the dead in the already over-crowded churchyards; and in 1854, Government ordered an inquiry into the matter. The result of an inspection of the various parochial burial-places in the city showed that they were in a worse state than in most other towns in the kingdom, and an order was issued to discontinue the practice of burying the dead therein as soon as possible. A Burial Board was formed; and after great deliberation, the Corporation selected a large plot of land on the Earlham Road, in that portion of Heigham now known as St. Philip's parish, as being the most suitable for the purposes of a Cemetery. It was commenced in 1855, and opened early in the following year, the first burial, if we do not reckon that of a workman who was accidentally killed in December, 1855, while engaged in the erection of one of the chapels, taking place on March 2nd, 1856. The eastern side of the Cemetery was consecrated by the Lord Bishop for the use of members of the Church of England;

while the remainder, except small portions set apart for the Roman Catholic and Jewish communities, was allotted to Dissenters.   The whole is prettily laid out, and planted with trees and shrubs.   The two principal chapels are in the Early English style of architecture, with porches and apsidal terminations ; while there is also a small chapel for the use of the Jews.   In February, 1877, a mortuary chapel for the Roman Catholics was consecrated.   The following statement shows the extent of land laid out in the Cemetery up to the present time :—*Consecrated :* February, 1856, 10 acres ; April, 1866, 7 acres ; March, 1875, 6 acres ; total, 23 acres. *Unconsecrated :* March, 1856, 10 acres ; January, 1879, 5 acres ; total, 15 acres.   Gross total, 38 acres.

On October 17th, 1878, a Soldiers' Monument or Memorial was unveiled at the Cemetery by Lord Waveney, in the presence of a large concourse of spectators.   The idea of erecting this memorial originated with a respected inhabitant of St. Philip's, Heigham, J. J. Winter, Esq.   In 1875, it was found necessary to enlarge the Cemetery by the addition of several acres of ground abutting on the Dereham Road, and the first grave dug thereon was for a soldier.   It occurred to Mr. Winter that it was desirable that a portion of this space should be set apart for the interment of soldiers who died while stationed at Norwich, and that a suitable memorial should be erected to their memory.   A committee was formed, of which Mr. Winter was appointed honorary secretary, and subscriptions solicited, amongst those contributing to the movement, in addition to most of the leading inhabitants of the city and county, being H.R.H. the Duke of Connaught, who had a year or two previously been located at Norwich with his regiment, the 7th Hussars.   The form of the memorial having been decided upon, the work was entrusted to Mr. John Bell, the celebrated sculptor of London, and a native of Norfolk. The monument, which is 21 feet in height, the figure being seven feet and the pedestal fourteen, has a very bold appearance. The figure forming the finial is of terra-cotta, and was cast by Messrs. Doulton, of the Lambeth Potteries, from Mr. Bell's design. It represents "The Spirit of the Army." On her sword sheath is seen a lion's head, designating strength; on her gorget there is a cross to point out the Christian soldier's faith; on her helmet the victor laurel; whilst the rose, shamrock, and thistle show that each portion of the United Kingdom contributes its quota to fill the ranks of the national army. The pedestal, which is six feet square, and is of the best Portland stone, was the work of F. Want and Sons, stonemasons, Heigham. It stands on a fine base consisting of one slab eight feet square, and on its front is inscribed the names of those soldiers whose remains have been interred on the spot. The memorial was very appropriately presented to Colonel Wake, of the 21st Hussars, as representing the British Army, that gallant officer's regiment, then stationed at Norwich, being present at the inauguration of the monument, which was a very interesting ceremony. Mr. Winter has in his possession a beautiful model of the original, presented to him by the distinguished sculptor.

THE NORWICH WORKHOUSE.

The Workhouse was erected in 1858-59, at a cost of £33,000, exclusive of £680 paid for a large plot of land which is cultivated by some of the inmates. It forms an extensive range of buildings in the Tudor style, and is capable of accommodating about 1000 paupers, although it never had so many inmates at one time. The institution formerly known as the Girls' Home, where orphan girls were trained for domestic service under the care of a matron, was a few years ago transferred to the Workhouse establishment. It was formerly carried on in an old building at the bottom of Holl's Lane (now Old Palace Road), the original Heigham Hall, but which is now used for the purposes of a brush manufactory.

THE CHURCH OF THE MOST HOLY TRINITY.

In the year 1859, through the strenuous exertions of the Rev. G. C. Hoste, M.A., then Rector of Heigham, and with the aid of a committee, of which Mr. J. J. Winter acted as the honorary secretary, it was decided, in order to supply the great want of church accommodation in the southern part of the hamlet, that a new church should be erected in Essex Street, Unthank's Road. The foundation stone was laid in August, 1859; and the building was consecrated on August 8th, 1861, by the Right Rev. the Lord Bishop, in the presence of the Mayor of Norwich, several members of the Corporation, and many ladies and gentlemen. The edifice is in the Decorated style of the fourteenth century, and is a commodious structure. It consists of a nave, two small transepts, and apsidal chancel, with a tower containing one bell, and surmounted by a slated spire rising to the height of about 120 feet. The interior of the building presents an extremely neat and handsome appearance. The pulpit and two reading desks are of oak, while there is also a lectern of the same material. On the walls on either side of the Communion Table have recently been placed two tablets, elegantly designed by Messrs. Pullen and Mase, of St. Giles', on which are inscribed the Decalogue and the Lord's Prayer and Creed. They were the gift of a parishioner. At the western end of the church has also been added a gallery for the accommodation during divine service of the children attending the Sunday School; while there are two rooms beneath which are used on ordinary occasions for choir practices and similar purposes. The church is capable of seating about 1100 persons. It was erected at a cost of £7000, including £700 paid for the site, the whole amount being covered by subscription. The church plate comprises a silver flagon, two chalices, and one paten, presented in 1861 by Lady Hoste and the Rev. W. R. Collett, M.A., Rector of Hethersett ; and a silver paten presented by J. C. Barnham, Esq. There is also a plated communion service.

ARCHÆOLOGICAL DISCOVERIES.

A discovery of considerable archæological interest was made in December, 1861, in a chalk pit a few yards from the public road, at Stone Hills, Heigham. Some laborers, while employed in what is locally termed "uncallowing," discovered, about four feet below the surface, a coffin of lead, evidently of great antiquity, which appeared to have been formerly enclosed in a wooden one. It was of simple construction, the lower portion being formed of one piece of lead, without solder or fastening ; the sides and ends merely turned up, and the top fitted in the same manner. No external ornamentation was visible. Within, the remains of a female skeleton were found. The jawbones were entire, and the teeth well preserved, the shape and enamel of the latter being very beautiful. Some pieces of mortar-like cement, and the bones of another skeleton, were found near. The dimensions of the coffin were—Length, 56 inches ; width at the head, 14 inches ; at the feet, 13 inches ; and the depth was 10 inches. It was probably of the Roman period. Mr. Fitch, F.S.A., &c., of The Woodlands, Dereham Road, who contributed an acount of this interesting discovery in a paper to the Norfolk and Norwich Archæological Society, from which he has kindly allowed us to

take these particulars, subsequently directed the workmen
to make a careful search for any ornaments, coins, or other
relics that might possibly have escaped their notice. After
some trouble, they found two bronze torque rings, of which
the engravings here given are the exact size. Both were

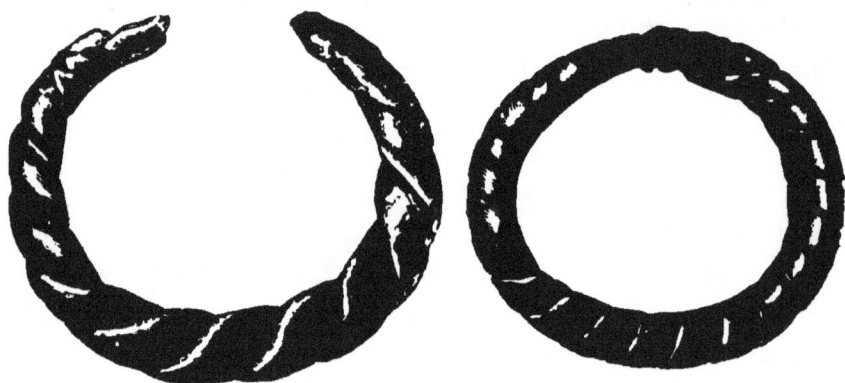

encrusted with a fine green patina, and were of beautiful
workmanship. The extremities were disunited, so that the
rings may be termed penannular; but it is probable that
the ends were originally soldered together. Whether they
were deposited with the skeleton found in the coffin could
not be ascertained. Mr. Fitch thought they were so enclosed,
but were thrown out by the workmen in the course of their
labors. The form, pattern, and workmanship led to the
conclusion that they were early Saxon. These remains were
found not many yards from the public road, a very usual
burial-place among the Romans. The ancient name of the
locality was Heigham Heath, and the land is copyhold of
the Bishop of Norwich.

A gold ring, as well as a brass coin of Faustina the Elder
(died A.D. 141), were subsequently found by Mr. Fitch in

Heigham, the latter on the same spot as the leaden coffin, and were exhibited by that gentleman at meetings of the Archæological Society.

By an Act of Parliament passed in 1863, for the purposes of the Norwich Union, the hamlet was divided into two distinct parishes, called North and South Heigham, the boundary line between the two districts being the Earlham Road.

In 1864, the Primitive Methodists erected a fine chapel on the Dereham Road, at a cost of about £1400. It is a substantial structure, capable of accommodating about 700 persons. The building was opened in October, 1864, since which time various alterations and improvements have been effected in it. There are also school and class rooms in connection with the chapel.

DIVISION OF THE HAMLET.

The Rev. G. C. Hoste, who was much beloved by his parishioners, resigned the Rectory of Heigham in 1865. His successor, the Rev. C. T. Rust, LL.B., in accordance with the expressed wishes of the Bishop, who has always evinced the greatest interest in Heigham, and in everything tending to the spiritual welfare of its inhabitants, proceeded to arrange with the Ecclesiastical Commissioners for the division of the hamlet into three distinct parishes, it having increased in population to such an extent as to render that course highly desirable. The population had risen from 5932 in 1841 to 7738 in 1851; while in 1861 it was 13,894.* South Heigham was already provided for; but the northern district was greatly in want of additional accommodation. Mr. Rust endeavored to meet this by hiring a room, capable of accommodating about 200 persons, which was licensed and opened for divine worship on the 1st of October, 1866, as the Heigham Mission Church. The hamlet being ripe for division, the southern portion of it was declared separate by an Order in Council dated the 5th of November, 1867. It was assigned to Trinity Church as a District Chapelry ; and on the 30th of April, 1868, it was declared a rectory. The new district was called

THE PARISH OF THE MOST HOLY
TRINITY, HEIGHAM.

It comprises all that part of Heigham which lies to the south of the Earlham Road, being bounded on the west by Earlham, on the south-west and south by Eaton and

---

* In 1871, the population had increased to 19,069,

Lakenham, on the east by a part of St. Stephen's parish and on the north by St. Philip's parish. Mr. Rust preferring to accept this new district, resigned the rectory of Heigham, and was licensed to his new sphere of labor on the 2nd of April, 1868. The living is a rectory, in the gift of the Bishop of Norwich, and is of the yearly value of £300. It is in the Deanery of Humbleyard, and 'Archdeaconry of Norfolk. The rector is the Rev. John Callis, M.A.; the churchwardens are Messrs. S. W. Corsbie and R. White. The parish has an estimated population of between 8000 and 9000.

The old Episcopal chapel is now converted into a National School for boys and infants, and it is also used as a Sunday School for South Heigham. The day schools were commenced in 1861, and are now attended by about 300 scholars. Mr. R. Adcock is the present master. There is no provision in the parish for the elementary instruction of girls.

THE BAPTIST CHURCH, UNTHANK'S ROAD.

The Baptist congregation formerly worshipping at St. Clement's Chapel, of which the celebrated Mark Wilks* was originally the pastor, decided a few years ago upon the erection of a new church on the Unthank's Road. The foundation stone was laid in July, 1874, by J. J. Colman, Esq., M.P.; and the building was opened for divine worship on the 8th of July, 1875. It is a large and handsome structure in the early Gothic style, with nave, aisles, and an apse. The building is 87 ft. long by 48 ft. 6 in. wide, the height of the nave being 46 feet. There are also school and

* This celebrated person, who "united the character of an Evangelical preacher with that of a sturdy and active politician," and was an excellent farmer, resided for some time at Heigham Hall, now the residence of J. F. Watson, Esq. Many quaint stories are narrated of him by some of the "ancient inhabitants" of that neighborhood.

class rooms beneath the church; but, as the floor of the principal structure is raised several feet above the surface of the land, they are well lighted and ventilated. Altogether, the cost of the edifice amounted to £6123, which has been nearly all raised by subscriptions.

SOUTH HEIGHAM PAROCHIAL HALL.

A Parochial Hall for South Heigham has been recently erected. The foundation stone was laid in July, 1877, by the Mayor of Norwich (R. Coller, Esq.), and the building was formally opened on the 4th of April, 1878, by the Lord Bishop. It was erected at a cost, including fittings, of upwards of £1400, and is used for the purposes of a Sunday School for girls, Bible classes, lectures, missionary and other meetings, and social gatherings. The building is a neat and substantial structure, and is situate in Essex Street, facing Trinity Church.

NORWICH CITY GAOL.

The building formerly used for the reception of the city prisoners stands in this parish, at the corner of Unthank's and St. Giles' Roads. Its erection was commenced in 1824, and finished in 1827, at a cost of upwards of £30,000. It is a large quadrangular building, and encloses an area of 1a. 2r. 34p. Two executions only took place here, the first being in August, 1829, when Stratford was publicly hung for poisoning; and the latter on the 20th of April, 1869, when William Sheward was privately executed within the walls of the prison for the murder of his wife in the year 1851. Under one of the previsions of the Prisons Act, 1877, the Gaol was closed in May of the year following, the prisoners being transferred to Norwich Castle; and the building will, we believe, soon be demolished.

THE PARISH OF ST. PHILIP, HEIGHAM,

was declared separate by an Order in Council gazetted March 31st, 1868, and was endowed by the Ecclesiastical Commissioners in the same year. It includes all that part of Heigham lying between the Earlham and Dereham Roads. The incumbency was offered to and accepted by the Rev. T. A. Nash, curate of St. Aldate, Oxford, who was licensed on the 21st of April, 1868. The living is a vicarage and perpetual curacy in the patronage of the Bishop of Norwich, and is valued at £300 yearly. It is in the Deanery of Humbleyard, and Norfolk Archdeaconry. When Mr. Nash took the parish, there was neither church, schools, nor any parochial organization whatever. He at once set to work to provide the necessary church accommodation, and through his liberality a large temporary church was erected near the City Road, St. Philip's. The edifice, which was built at the sole cost of Mr. Nash, and afterwards presented by him to the parish, was opened in February, 1869. It was used as a place for divine worship until the completion of a more convenient structure in Heigham Road, and was capable of seating about six hundred persons. The building is now converted into a Sunday School, and is well filled every Sunday. It is also used during the week as a Young Men's Society room, and for the purposes of anniversary and other meetings.

ST. PHILIP'S CHURCH.

A committee was then formed to raise funds to erect a new church, consisting of the Vicar, Mr. J. J. Winter, Mr. F. J. Page, Mr. C. Thorn, and others. It was commenced in May, 1870. The foundation stone was laid on July 6th of the same year, by A. F. C. Bolingbroke, Esq., Mayor

of Norwich, in the presence of the Sheriff, the Dean, and
many ladies and gentlemen.   The edifice was consecrated
on the 3rd of August, 1871, by the Lord Bishop.   It is in
the early French style of the 13th century, and has north
and south aisles, chancel, nave, vestry, and organ chamber on
the northern side.   There is also a narthex or western porch,
and a baptistry is formed by the tower being placed at the
west angle.   The building is faced with flint.   Internally,
the church presents a handsome appearance.   The pulpit is
of carved oak, and was the 'gift of Miss Edwards.   There is
a reading desk of the same material, which was presented by
the members of the Young Men's Bible Class and some of
the elder scholars.   The reredos, which is of Caen stone, and
very handsome, was the gift of the esteemed curate of the
parish, the Rev. C. L. Rudd (now vicar of Hempstead), and
his Bible class.   The church, the site for which was given
by the late George Gedge, Esq., is capable of accommodating
about 800 persons.   It was erected at a cost of about
£5000, which was covered by subscription, the Bishop giving
£1000 towards it.   This amount, however, does not include
an estimated outlay of £1800 for the completion of the
tower and spire, of which only about one-third was erected
at the time the church was built.

The church plate comprises a silver flagon, two cups, and
a paten, purchased by subscription; two additional cups,
presented by the Misses Scott, of Colney Hall; and two
additional patens presented by the Rev. T. A. and Mrs.
Nash, one in memory of their infant son, and the other
of Mrs. Nash's mother.

ST. PHILIP'S DAY SCHOOLS.

The work of completing the tower and spire to the newly-
erected church was interrupted at the outset owing to the

ST. PHILIP'S CHURCH.
(As Designed.)

urgent necessity which existed of at once building suitable schools for the parish, and in order to secure a grant from Government. The erection of the schools was decided upon in 1870, at a time when the citizens of Norwich were engaged in discussing the merits of Mr. Forster's Education Act. A committee was formed, of which the Rev. T. A. Nash was appointed chairman, and the appeal they made was well responded to by the friends of voluntary education. The schools were opened on the 14th of November, 1872, and cost (with the site) over £2000. They are situate on Paragon Hill, and were designed to accommodate about 400 children. Miss Simpson is mistress of the girls', and Miss Wilkinson of the infants' school ; while the boys are under the mastership of Mr. Driver. The schools from the commencement have been well attended, and are generally considered to be one of the best group of schools in Norwich. Over the fireplace in the Boys' School-room is a stone with the following inscription :—

The St. Philip's, Heigham, Schools for Boys, Girls, and Infants, were erected in the year 1872, the expense having been chiefly borne by the parishioners, aided by the sum of £900 contributed by James Harford, Esq., and Miss Harford, for the purpose of securing to the children of this parish an open Bible and a Christian education.

> T. A. NASH, M.A., *Vicar.*
> C. L. RUDD, M A., *Curate.*
> J. J. WINTER, } *Churchwardens.*
> F. J. PAGE,

The task of erecting the schools having been accomplished, the parishioners next turned their attention to the completion of the tower and spire. In 1875 an appeal was made for subscriptions, which resulted in £450 being raised. Further efforts, however, were postponed, so as not to hinder the movement which had been commenced in St. Bartholomew's parish for the restoration and enlargement of the old church. That having been accomplished, another effort was made on

New Year's Day, 1879, when a large committee was formed, with the respected vicar and curate, the Rev. S. Linton and the Rev. II. Pelham (son of the Lord Bishop), as chairman and honorary secretary, and Mr. J. J. Winter as treasurer. A canvass of the parish, with some liberal donations from friends outside, resulted in realising about £1000 out of the £1800 required. and the tower is now being completed by Messrs. Lacey, of Norwich. The committee earnestly hope that the remaining £800 may be forthcoming, to enable them to complete the spire also, and thus save the expense of scaffolding, which will prove a serious item in the cost at any future time if once removed. One ground of appeal they have put forward for aid from all Norwich is that the Cemetery lies in St. Philip's parish, and it is suggested that the relatives and friends of those buried there should make this a Memorial Tower and Spire. Mrs. Palmer, of West Parade, Earlham Road, has generously promised, a handsome clock for the tower, in memory of her late husband, and this will prove a great boon to the neighborhood.

There is a chapel belonging to the Wesleyan Reformers in this parish. It was opened in April, 1860, and is a plain but substantial structure, with white-brick front. The building cost about £500, and will seat 300 persons.

THE PARISH OF ST. BARTHOLOMEW, HEIGHAM.

· The old parish of St. Bartholomew, which contained an estimated population at the division of the hamlet in 1868 of 6000 persons, was left sadly in want of adequate church accommodation. The only provision for the spiritual welfare of its inhabitants was a mere village church at the extreme north-western corner of the parish, with roads leading to it almost impassable in wet weather, and a Mission Room at the eastern end, the two places together being capable of seating not more than 400 persons. Taking advantage of a convenient opportunity, the Mission Room, which is at present used for the purposes of a Working Men's Club, &c., was purchased in 1868 at a cost of £420. The next step decided upon was the erection of a temporary church in Adelaide Street, in the very centre of the district. It was built upon a plot of land which originally formed part of a garden attached to a house purchased some time previously by the Ecclesiastical Commissioners as a parsonage house for the benefice. The edifice, which cost over £800, and affords accommodation for 500 persons, was opened on the 29th of November, 1870.

ST. BARTHOLOMEW'S CHURCH.

At a parish meeting in July, 1876, the Rector presiding, it was unanimously resolved, on the motion of J. F. Watson, Esq., of Heigham Hall, seconded by J. J. Winter, Esq., of St. Philip's, that the old parish church, which was in a very dilapidated condition, should be restored and enlarged to afford increased accommodation for the parishioners, and as a memorial to Bishop Hall, whose remains were interred here in 1656. A committee was formed, with the Rector, the Rev. F. Taylor, as chairman, to raise the necessary funds, and a bazaar was held in St. Andrew's Hall, in aid thereof, in 1878. The old church was a very ancient structure, and consisted, as we have elsewhere stated, of a nave, south aisle, tower, and vestry. The principal part of the edifice, in the opinion of R. M. Phipson, Esq., to whom the work of restoration and enlargement was entrusted, was erected

early in the fifteenth century, some time during the reigns
of Henry V. or VI.   The plans prepared by Mr. Phipson,
and approved by the parish and other authorities, included
the restoration of the existing nave, aisle, and tower; the
removal of the old porch and vestry; and the building of
a north aisle, with organ chamber and vestry.   The work
was quickly proceeded with; and on April 26th, 1878, a
memorial stone was laid by the Rector, in the presence of a
number of ladies and gentlemen, including J. F. Watson,
Esq., R. Fitch, Esq., J.P., and others.   The stone bears the
following inscription :—

"To the glory of God, and in memory of Bishop Hall, and of the
enlargement and complete restoration of the Church of St. Bartholomew,
Heigham, this stone was laid on the 26th of April, A.D. 1878.

FREDERICK TAYLOR, <i>Rector.</i>

CHARLES SCARLE,   }
JOHN CROSS,   }   <i>Churchwardens.</i>

The edifice was re-opened on December 12th, 1878.   It
presents a strangely-altered appearance, which is especially
noticeable in the internal arrangements.   It is capable of
seating about 400 persons, and the whole of the seats are free.
The pulpit and reading desk are of oak.   The Communion
Table, which is handsomely carved, was the gift of the Rev.
Canon Hinds Howell, of Drayton, and has the following
legend round it :—

Hinds Howell, clerk, M.A., Rector of Drayton, dedicated this altar
table to Almighty God, A.D. 1878, in memory of Joseph Hall, D.D.,
Lord Bishop of Norwich, who died in 1656, but whose virtues and
learning, as also the persecution which he endured, still linger in the
hearts of English Churchmen.

In the nave there is an octagonal font of ancient date, and
of a pattern said to be common in Norfolk in the fifteenth
century.

The entire cost of the alterations, including heating and
lighting, the construction of new and more convenient

approaches to the church, and the making of some desirable improvements in the churchyard, amounted to upwards of £3000, all of which is now cleared off, a result owing partly to the liberality of J. F. Watson, Esq.

The living is a rectory, in the gift of the Bishop of Norwich, and is valued at £300 yearly. It is in the Deanery of Humbleyard, and the Archdeaconry of Norfolk. The parish has an estimated population of 8000, and comprises all that part of Heigham lying between the Dercham Road and the Back River, by which it is bounded on the north, with the exception of several fields on the other side of the stream, which are included in Heigham. It extends to Hellesdon and Earlham on the west, and is bounded on the south by St. Philip's parish, and on the east by the city of Norwich.

The church plate is of ancient date, and comprises two silver chalices and a paten. One of the chalices is dated 1567, and has inscribed on the cover, "SENT BARTELMEUS OF HAYHAM;" the other is dated 1707, and was presented by a former rector, the Rev. J. Whitefoot, M.A., who was also minister of St. Peter's Mancroft and St. Gregory's Churches, a Commissary of Norwich Archdeaconry, and a Clerk of Convocation. The chalice has this inscription :—"ECCLAE·STI· BARTHOLMEI DE HEGHAM JUXTA NORVIC, SACRUM. J. W., Rr." The paten is dated 1656.

The chief feature of interest in connection with this church lies in its association with the memory of Bishop Hall; for here the pious Bishop, on his retirement to Heigham after the persecutions he endured, preached many of those quaint but homely sermons for which he was so celebrated. In another part of this little work will be found a brief account of his life. On the wall on the south side of the chancel is a curious mural monument to the Bishop's memory, whereupon is represented a golden figure of Death, holding in his

right hand a scroll on which is inscribed :—" DEBEMUS
MORTI NOS NOSTRAQUE." Upon another paper in his left
hand are the words, " PERSOLVIT ET QUIETUS EST ;" and
between the legs of the figure, " OBIJT. 8 SEPTEM., ANO.
ÆRÆ. XIANE. 1656, ÆT: SUÆ. 82." At the foot of the
monument is inscribed :—" JOSEPHVS HALLVS, OLIM HUMILIS
ECCLESIÆ SERVUS." The following is a translation :—

"We owe to death both ourselves and our property. He has paid
the debt, and is released. He died 8th of September, in the year of the
Christian Æra 1656, the 82nd year of his age. JOSEPH HALL, once a
humble servant of the Church."

Bishop Hall's Monument.

There was in former times a gravestone to Bishop Hall's
memory beneath this monument ; and in other parts of the
edifice were stones in remembrance of Elizabeth, the "deare
and virtuous consort of Joseph Hall," who died in 1652,
and of their son, Edward Hall.

There is a brass in this edifice to Thomas Holl, Esq., who was probably a courtier of the time of Charles the First. Blomefield says the family of Holl or Holly was originally seated at Aylsham, Norfolk. Cotman noticed this brass in his work on " The Brasses of Norfolk," and it formerly had the following inscription attached to it :—

Here lieth the body of Thomas Holl, second sonne to Thomas Holl, Esquire, who was buried the 6th of March, 1630.

In this church there is also a handsome mural monument to Thomas Seaman, Esq., a benefactor to Heigham as well as to other parishes in the city of Norwich ; and monuments to other persons of note in their time. There are also neat tablets to the memory of William Unthank, Esq., and Mrs. Unthank, as well as of their son, William Samuel Unthank, who was killed at the siege of Badajoz, April 7th, 1812. Other stones bear inscriptions to members of the Parr, Hanger, Haylett, Smith, and Robbins families. In the churchyard lie the remains of William Arderon, F.R.S., a distinguished naturalist, who died November 25th, 1767, as is testified by a neat monument erected to his memory in the church. In early life he was managing clerk at the New Mills. He published many valuable works on Natural History subjects.

During the work of restoration, a large stone coffin was dug up in the nave just below where the pulpit formerly stood. A lid was also found, which was nearly a foot shorter than the coffin, and it is doubtful whether it ever belonged thereto. It is, however, possible that it did so belong, and that a separate piece of stone was originally placed over the head. The coffin had evidently been reduced in depth by the chipping away of the upper portions of its sides, so that it seemed too shallow for the reception of a body. There was no inscription or ornamentation about the coffin to give

any clue as to whose body had been lodged in it.   It has
been placed near the mural monument to Thomas Seaman,
Esq.

Beneath the plaster-work on the south side of the chancel
a piscina was found, which had doubtless in ancient times,
before King Henry the Eighth issued his fiat for the dissolution of the monasteries, been used by many a priest of the
Church of Rome.   It has been restored, and inserted in the
wall close to its original position, near the communion
rails. Some silver and copper coins of the period of Charles
I. were also picked up during the restoration of the edifice.
Several fragments of brass inscriptions were also found, which
were exhibited by Mr. Fitch, F.S.A., at a meeting of the
Archæological Society.

HEIGHAM STREET BOARD SCHOOLS.

The Norwich School Board, shortly after its formation in
1871, decided upon the erection of suitable school buildings
for children residing in the densely-populated district of
North Heigham.   These schools, which were the first built
in Norwich by the Board, are situate in Heigham Street, and
are of red brick, ornamented by black bands.   The buildings
form a quadrangle, enclosing a spacious playground for the
girls and infants, the boys' recreation ground being at the
rear.   The Boys' School was opened late in 1873 ; and the
Girls' and Infants' Schools in January, 1874.   The number
of children on the books is greatly in excess of that for
which there is accommodation.

IN MEMORIAM—JAMES WINTER, ESQ.

This gentleman, who was universally esteemed, resided in
Heigham for many years, and was for a long time one of the
Councillors for West Wymer Ward, in which the parish is

situate. He held the office of Chairman of the Court of Guardians, and also filled the important position of Speaker in the old Norwich Corporation. On the breaking up of that body in 1835 he was presented with a massive silver epergne, on which was inscribed the following :—

Presented by the Corporation of Norwich to James Winter, Esq., Speaker of the Common Council, in testimony of their high respect for the impartial manner in which he has discharged the important duties of his office, and for the services he has upon all occasions rendered to his fellow-citizens.—1835.

Mr. Winter removed to Drayton Lodge, Norfolk, in 1859, where he died, February 16, 1876, aged 79.

The Norwich Steam Laundry and Baths Company (Limited) in 1878 decided upon the construction of extensive laundry premises and a swimming bath in North Heigham, on a site where Norton's Bath House formerly stood, adjacent to the river, and in a neighborhood known upwards of a century ago as the Heigham Bleaching Ground. The laundry buildings are of red brick, and form an extensive range of premises, next the road. The laundry is now in full working order, and will prove, like similar institutions in other large towns, of great convenience to large families in Norwich. The swimming bath, which is estimated to cost about £1500, is now nearly completed. It is 75 feet long by 25 feet wide, with a depth of 3 feet at one end and of 6 feet at the other. The facilities which the Company have in their laundry for heating water will enable them to provide a tepid swimming bath in the colder months of the year. S. Culley, Esq., is Secretary to the Company.

Under one of the provisions of an Act of Parliament known as the "Norwich Improvement Act, 1879," the city authorities are empowered to construct a new road and bridge in Heigham, for carriage traffic and foot passengers, com-

mencing opposite Russell Street, and from thence crossing
the river and terminating in St. Martin-at-Oak Street,
opposite Baker's Road.   We hope this long-talked-of project
will soon be realised, as it will prove of great convenience
to the inhabitants on both sides of the river, and to· the
citizens generally.

The Primitive Methodists have recently erected a neat
chapel in this parish.   It is situate in Nelson Street.   The
foundation stone was laid by J. J. Colman, Esq., M.P., in
November, 1878, and the chapel opened in August, 1879.

THE DOLPHIN INN—BISHOP HALL'S PALACE.

The old flint-faced building now called the Dolphin Inn,
but once the residence of Bishop Hall, has much in it to
attract the notice of the antiquarian and archæologist. Before
the house stands the ornamental gateway, just as in the
Bishop's time.   The house is of the character of the architecture of the time of James I., having two projecting bays,
one on each side of the door.   These were doubtless thrown
out in 1615, as indicated by the date upon them.   Over
the ornamental doorway is the date "1587;" and in the
corners are the initials and merchant's mark of one Richard
Browne, whose residence it apparently was some time during
the 16th century.   In the wall at the entrance are the
remains of a piscina, or place for holy water, within a
beautifully sculptured niche.   The principal room of the
house has wood pannelled ornamental walls, oak doors, and
an elaborately plastered ceiling, all of the Jacobean period.
It was probably the general hall of the family.   Patrick,
afterwards Bishop of Ely, is said to have been ordained in
this room by Bishop Hall.   It is much to be regretted that
this ancient building, wherein the good Bishop passed the
latter years of his life, cannot be rescued from the somewhat

degrading associations with which in modern times it has
become invested.   We have heard it suggested by a leading
Churchman in Norwich that, if restored, it could be converted into an excellent residence for the Rector of Heigham;
and we trust that, should the opportunity arise, some such
plan will be carried out.   A great improvement has been
effected in the appearance of this neighborhood within the
last year or two.

Bishop Hall's Palace (now the Dolphin Inn.)

FLOODS IN HEIGHAM.

The low-lying parts of Heigham, like other districts of Norwich adjacent to the river, have at various times suffered greatly from the devastating effects of floods. Blomefield gives an instance of one occurring as early as in the 13th century; and again in the 14th and 16th centuries great damage was done. In 1614, 1646, and 1673 there were also great floods, and several other inundations followed in quick succession. On December 31st, 1734, was "the greatest flood known in Norwich since 1696. All [Lower] Heigham was under water." Well-recorded instances are also given of other inundations occurring in 1737, 1739 (when there was a "prodigious flood,") and 1740. The *Norfolk and Norwich Remembrancer* says, "On October 27th, 1762, occurred a sudden flood in Norwich, which laid nearly 300 houses and eight parish churches under water. It rose twelve feet perpendicular in twenty-four hours." In 1770 there was another flood, three inches lower than the preceding one. On November 6th, 1794, according to the *Remembrancer*, "a sudden and rapid flood occasioned great distress to the poor inhabitants of Heigham and the lower parts of the city. Boats were rowed in several streets." Again, in February, 1795, after heavy falls of snow, a rapid thaw produced an almost general inundation, and the poor inhabitants of Heigham and the lower parts of the city were a second time reduced to a state of great distress. On January 28th, 1809, another flood ensued upon a thaw, when the lower parts of the city were deluged. Boats were rowed in St. Martin's-at-Oak street, and some of the houses were six or seven feet under water.

Although the waters generally covered the same area, yet none of the inundations we have referred to caused such widespread misery and destruction of property as that which occurred on November 16th and 17th, 1878, owing to the fact that what was in former times chiefly waste or meadow land had then become densely populated. The latter part of the autumn of 1878 was marked by exceptionally heavy rainfalls, followed by severe snowstorms. A rapid thaw set in, and the various brooklets and tributaries of the Wensum, which takes its rise in the north-western part of Norfolk, near West Rudham, became swollen to a great extent. Grave fears were entertained of an impending disaster, which culminated in actual alarm on the 16th of November, on its becoming known that the usually insignificant stream called the Back River had considerably overflown the marshes on either side, and that the waters, held back by the New Mills, were rapidly spreading towards Heigham Causeway. The Mills, as on previous occasions, proved an obstruction to the tide, although Mr. Wells, the tenant, opened every aperture beneath them in order to allow the waters to escape. St. Martin's, on the one side, was rapidly submerged; and on the other, Heigham Street and the Causeway were converted into a deep river, the waters spreading up the various streets branching off from those localities, thereby flooding the lower rooms of many habitations in the district, so that the inmates had to seek refuge in their bed-rooms. During the night the waters rose considerably, and on the 17th (Sunday) they extended to the bottom of Old Palace Road, there being a depth of between six and seven feet on the Causeway. The numerous streets leading from Dereham Road into Heigham Street were rendered impassable, the lower parts of Tinkler's Lane, Napier Street, Derby Street, and other localities, being flooded to a considerable depth, and the poor people, as in other parts of the city, compelled to seek refuge in the upper part of their dwellings. The

work of rescuing the unfortunate sufferers was proceeded
with in good earnest, hundreds of ready helpers doing their
utmost, by means of boats, carts, and waggons, to rescue
them from their perilous position.   Energetic measures were
also speedily taken by the Mayor of Norwich (H. Bullard,
Esq.), the Sheriff (D. Steward, Esq.), and the leading citizens,
for the relief of the really necessitous, and several public
buildings as well as numerous private houses were thrown
open for the accommodation of those rendered homeless by
the disaster.   A public subscription was also made in aid of
the sufferers, which resulted in the handsome sum of £5428
being raised.   The waters commenced subsiding on Sunday
evening, the 17th of November, and by the 20th they had
entirely disappeared from the flooded districts.   Two lives
were, sad to narrate, unfortunately lost in Heigham by this
terrible flood.*

* In the wall of the New Mill Yard is a stone showing the heights to
which the waters have risen in previous years. The city authorities would
do well to insert the date marked (†).   The stone is four feet high.

1614————

1646————
† Nov. 17th, 1878————

1762————

1770————

1734————

RECTORS.

The following is a list of the Rectors of Heigham from 1313 to the present year (1879) :—

	A.D.		A.D.
John de Hoveton -	1313	John Morgan - -	1573
William de Broke -	1314	Thomas Plumb - -	1585
Alexander de Berneye -	1320	Paul Chapman, A.M. -	1600
Sylvester atte Gates -	1327	Thomas Stokes, A.M. -	1630
John de Thefford -	1354	John Whitefoot, sen. -	1652
Robt. Kenton { mentioned as Rector }	1377	John Whitefoot, jun. -	1682
		Anthony Aufrere, A.M.-	1731
Roger Pratt - -	1397	Robert Parr - - -	1781
John Popy - -	1443	Wm. Farley Wilkinson, } M.A. - - - }	1812
John Aylesham - -	1445		
Robert Popy - -	1449	*Thomas Sugden Talbot, } M.A. - - - }	1813
Simon Thornham -	1454		
Hugh Acton - -	1454	Robert Bathurst, M.A. -	1828
Thomas Folkard - -	1455	John Prowett, M.A. -	1829
Richard Brakeburgh -	1461	William Robbins, M A.-	1833
John Munde - -	1465	George Charles Hoste, } M.A. - - - }	1856
Elias Bartram - -	1504		
John Thuxton - -	1517	Cyprian Thomas Rust, } LL.B. - - - }	1865
Cornelius Bals - -	1523		
William Paye, A.M. -	1526	Jno. Gilbert Dixon, B.A.	1868
William Askoe or Ascew	1555	Frederick Taylor, M.A.	1875

Rectors of the District or new Parish of the Most Holy Trinity, Heigham.

Cyprian Thomas Rust, LL.B. -	- †licensed 2nd April 1868
John Callis, M.A. - - -	- instituted 28th May 1875

Vicars or Perpetual Curates of the District or new Parish of St. Philip, Heigham.

Thomas Augustus Nash, M.A. -	- licensed 21st April 1868
Sydney Linton, M.A. - - -	- ,, 1st August 1877

* Instituted a second time in 1817.
+ The living was legally declared to be a Rectory, 30th April, 1868.

THE CHARITIES.

Heigham, the largest suburb of Norwich, has fewer charities than any other parish in the city. Robert Powell, by will dated 1675, charged an estate in Heigham with the annual payment of £1, to be divided equally amongst forty poor widows on St. Thomas' Day.

Thomas Seaman, of Heigham, Esq., Sheriff of Norwich in 1679, and some time High Sheriff of Norfolk, by his last will and testament dated 10th of August, 1700, gave and devised to his eldest son, Peter Seaman, his heirs and assigns, a close of land containing twenty acres, lying in the parish of Earlham, subject to the payment of the clear yearly sum of £10, on the Feast of the Annunciation of the Blessed Virgin Mary, to the churchwardens or overseers of the poor of the parishes of Heigham, St. Benedict, St. Swithin's, and St. Margaret, Norwich, or of any two of the said parishes, for the binding and putting forth apprentice every year for ever two poor boys whose parents shall be dwelling in any two of the said parishes. Mr. Seaman also gave and devised to his second son, Thomas Seaman, a close of land in Heigham, subject to the payment of the clear yearly sum of £5, on the same day and to the same parties and parishes as in the former bequest, for the binding forth apprentice every year for ever two poor girls of any two of the parishes referred to.

Ann Parr, by codicils annexed to her last will, in 1816 bequeathed to two trustees, of whom the Rector of Heigham for the time being should be one, the sum of £1500 Three per Cent. Reduced Stock, upon trust, to divide the annual dividends thereof on the 1st of December in every year for ever in equal shares amongst six poor men and six poor women resident in Heigham, of the age of 70 years and upwards, or to apply the same to their benefit, at the discretion of the trustees. From this stock, the sum of £146 13s. was sold out for payment of the legacy duty, leaving the balance £1353 18s. 9d., the annual dividends of which amount to £40 12s. 4d., and admit of the distribution of £3 7s. 8¼d. to each of the objects of the charity.

BISHOP HALL.

The following brief memoir of this distinguished prelate will prove interesting to the reader :—

JOSEPH HALL, generally called "our English Seneca," was born on the 1st of July, 1574, at Bristow Park, in the parish of Ashby-de-la-Zouch, Leicestershire. His parentage was highly respectable, his father being an officer serving under the religious Earl of Huntingdon, and his mother was a woman of great piety. Hall was educated by a private tutor until he attained the age of fifteen years, when he was sent to Cambridge University, and admitted to Emmanuel College, where he gained a Fellowship, and was chosen Professor of Rhetoric two years in succession. In 1597 he published his *Virgidemiarum*, or "Satires," in six books, which were re-printed at Oxford in 1753. Pope said of this work that it was "the best poetry and the truest satire in the English language." Subsequently, he entered into holy orders, and in 1601 was appointed to the Rectory of Halstead, in Suffolk. About two years later he was married to Elizabeth, a daughter of Mr. George Winniffe, of Brettenham, Suffolk. Hall afterwards travelled on the Continent, and at Brussels engaged in a discussion with a celebrated Jesuit of that city, one Father Costerus, in which he stoutly defended the truths of his own faith. It is related of this discussion that when the Popish priest would fain have proceeded in praise of his Church, Hall stopped his boasting by saying, "Sir, I beseech you, mistake me not; my nation tells you of what religion I am." Having spent a year and a-half in these travels, Hall returned to London, where Prince Henry chanced to hear him preach, and was so pleased with his discourse that he appointed him as his chaplain. He was next presented to the Rectory of Waltham Abbey, in Essex ; and subsequently made a Prebendary of Wolverhampton and Dean of Worcester. Hall was then deputed by the King, together with four other learned English divines, to attend a General Synod at Dort, in the Netherlands, in order to aid in settling some theological disputes. He was, however, obliged to return to England after a stay of two or three months, in consequence of ill-health, the States before he took his departure presenting him with a gold medal, as a mark of the high estimation in which they held his learning.

On returning to his native country, Hall soon recovered his health. About the year 1624 he was offered the Bishopric of Gloucester, which

he refused; but in 1627 he was elevated to the see of Exeter, whence on
November 15th, 1641, he was translated to that of Norwich. This was
at a time when there were severe conflicts between the different parties
in Church and State; and in the disputes which arose between Charles
the First and the Parliament, such was the popular feeling against those
of the episcopal order, that the Bishops were mobbed in the streets of
London, and were prevented from taking their seats in the House of
Lords. Twelve of their number, including the Archbishop of York and
Bishop Hall, accordingly drew up a protest against the validity of such
laws as might be made during their compulsory absence from Parliament;
and being accused by the Commons of high treason, they were ordered
to be committed to the Tower, whither they were taken one cold night
in the depth of winter. The charge of high treason was, however,
subsequently withdrawn, and Hall and his brethren were ordered to be
discharged; but upon another pretext they were again sent to the Tower,
where they were kept in confinement for upwards of six months, Hall
and his companions being finally liberated, upon each giving bail for
£5000, in June, 1642.

Bishop Hall immediately withdrew to Norwich, where he was, to quote
from his own work appropriately entitled "Hard Measure," "at first
received with more respect than in such times I could have expected.
There I preached the day after my arrival, to a numerous and attentive
people; neither was sparing of my pains in this kind ever since, till the
times, growing every day more impatient of a Bishop, threatened my
silencing." Troublous times, indeed, were those for men of his sacred
order, as well as for many other persons. Bishop Hall was one of the
first to fall under the lash of the dominant party, although he had at
one time been suspected of a leaning towards the Puritans. Early in
1643, an ordinance was passed for sequestrating the estates of notorious
"Papists and delinquents," and the good Bishop was included amongst
the number, his property being seized, the rents of his bishopric stopped,
and the sanctity of the palace violated. The whole of his effects and
books were ordered to be sold at a public auction, and would have been
so disposed of had not two of the Bishop's friends kindly gave bond for
the amount of the valuation. "Yea, they would have appraised our
very wearing clothes," says the Bishop, "had not Alderman Tooley and
Sheriff Rawley, to whom I sent to require their judgment concerning the
ordinance in this point, declared their opinion to the contrary." The
Parliamentary Committee sitting at Norwich, on an appeal from the
Bishop to be allowed some means out of the Church's patrimony for
his maintenance, afterwards "set out so many of the manors belonging
to the bishopric as should amount to the sum of £400 annually;" but
this was countermanded by those at London, at the instigation of Miles
Corbet the regicide, and an order granted for a fifth part of the revenues
of the see to be allowed the Bishop's wife "for the sustentation of herself
and family," the sequestrators telling Hall they could not allow him
anything. Some difficulty was experienced in ascertaining what this
"fifth part" amounted to, as no accounts could be obtained for a
considerable time of the rents and revenues of the bishopric, which had
been appropriated by the sequestrators; and when at length an account

was furnished, it was so "confused", and "imperfect" that, to use the Bishop's own words, "we could never come to know what a fifth part meant, so they were content that I should eat my books, by setting off the sum engaged for them out of the fifth part."

"In the meantime," continues the Bishop, "the synodals both in Norfolk and Suffolk, and all the spiritual profits of the diocese, were also kept back; only ordinations and institutions continued awhile. But after the Covenant was appointed to be taken, and was generally swallowed of both clergy and laity, my power of ordination was, with some strange violence, restrained; for when I was going on in my wonted course, which no law or ordinance had inhibited, certain forward volunteers in the city, banding together, stir up the Mayor and Aldermen and Sheriffs to call me to an account for an open violation of their Covenant. To this purpose, divers of them came to my gates at a very unseasonable time, and knocking very vehemently, required to speak with the Bishop. Messages were sent to them to know their business: nothing would satisfy them but the Bishop's presence. At last I came down to them, and demanded what the matter was: they would have the gate opened, and then they would tell me. I answered that I would know them better first; if they had anything to say to me I was ready to hear them. They told me they had a writing to me from Mr. Mayor and some other of their magistrates. The paper contained both a challenge of me for breaking the Covenant, in ordaining ministers, and, withal, required me to give in the names of those which were ordained by me both then and formerly since the Covenant. My answer was, that Mr. Mayor was much abused by those who had misinformed him, and drawn that paper from him; that I would the next day give a full answer to the writing. They moved that my answer might be by my personal appearance at the Guildhall. I asked them when they ever heard of a Bishop of Norwich appearing before a Mayor. I knew mine own place, and would take that way of answer which I thought fit; and so dismissed them, who had given out that day that had they known before of mine ordaining, they would have pulled me and those whom I ordained out of the chapel by the ears.

"While I received nothing, yet something was required of me. They were not ashamed, after they had taken away and sold all my goods and personal estate, to come to me for assessments and monthly payments for that estate which they had taken; and took distresses from me upon my most just denial; and vehemently required me to find the wonted arms of my predecessors, when they had left me nothing."

The Bishop and his family had during this time to put up with many "insolencies and affronts." "One while," he says, "a whole rabble of volunteers came to my gates late, when they were locked up, and called for the porter to give them entrance, which being not yielded, they threatened to make by force; and had not the said gates been very strong, they had done it. Others of them clambered over the walls, and would come into my house; their errand, they said, was to search for delinquents. What they would have done I know not, had not we by a secret way sent to raise the officers for our rescue." In 1644, it was ordered by the Court sitting at Norwich that "Sheriff Toftes, Mr. Lindsey, Mr. Puckle, and others, shall from time to time meet together and repair to the several churches in this city and view the same, and take notice of such scandalous pictures, crucifixes, and images, as are yet remaining in the same churches." Sheriff Toftes and Alderman Lindsey, with many zealous followers, accordingly went to the Bishop's chapel to look for what they termed " superstitous pictures and relics of idolatry." They insisted on the demolition of the windows, which were filled, they said, with offensive images. The Bishop explained, that these images were "pictures of some ancient and worthy bishops, as St. Ambrose, Austin, &c.," to which they replied that they were so many Popes. However, the Bishop having promised to remove the heads of the figures, they consented that the bodies might remain. Bishop Hall in the work we have before referred to, and from which we have quoted somewhat copiously, narrates what afterwards occurred :—" It is no other than tragical to relate the carriage of that furious sacrilege, whereof our eyes and ears were the sad witnesses, under the authority and presence of Lindsey, Toftes the sheriff, and Greenwood. Lord, what work was here ! what clattering of glasses ; what beating down of walls ; what tearing up of monuments ; what pulling down of seats ; what wresting out of irons and brass from the windows and graves ; what defacing of arms ; what demolishing of curious stonework, that had not any representation in the world, but only of the cost of the founder and skill of the mason ; what tooting and piping upon the destroyed organ pipes ; and what a hideous triumph on the market day before all the country, when, in a kind of sacrilegious and profane procession, all the organ pipes, vestments, both copes and surplices, together with the leaden cross which had been newly sawn down from over the Green Yard pulpit, and the service books and singing books that could be had, were carried to the fire in the public Market-place ; a lewd wretch, walking before the train, in his cope trailing in the dirt, with a service book in his hand, imitating in an impious scorn the tune, and usurping the words of the Litany used formerly in the church. Near the public cross all ' these monuments of idolatry ' must be sacrificed to the fire ; not without much ostentation of a zealous joy, in discharging ordnance, to the cost of some who professed how much they had longed to see that day. Neither was it any news upon this guild-day, to have the cathedral, now open on all sides, to be filled with musketeers, waiting for the Mayor's return, drinking and tobacconing as freely as if it had turned alehouse."

At length the Bishop was thrust out of his palace by a peremptory order ; and " so we might, he says, have lain in the street for ought I know, had not the providence of God so ordered it that a neighbor in the Close, one Mr. Gostlin, a widower, was content to void his house for us. This hath been my Measure ; wherefore, I know not. Lord, Thou knowest, who only canst remedy and end, and forgive or avenge this horrible oppression.—Jos. Norvic, scripsi, May 29th, 1647."

The Bishop eventually removed to Heigham, the sequestration having been taken off a small estate which he rented there. The house in which he found shelter still exists, and is an old flint and stone building, with deep bay windows and pointed gables, now used for the purpose of a public-house, called the " Dolphin Inn." We have briefly noticed this interesting building in another part of this little work.' Here the good Bishop passed the remaining years of a long life in comparative quietness and peace, broken only as they were by the death of his beloved partner, which occurred in August, 1652. The sufferings he had undergone do not appear to have damped his courage, for he exerted himself in his old age even as in the prime of his life to do all the good that lay in his power. In the parish where he last lived, he gave a weekly contribution of money to certain poor widows to his dying day. "It was well known," said his friend, the Rev. John Whitefoot, M.A., Rector of Heigham, in a funeral sermon on the Bishop, preached in St. Peter's Mancroft Church, September 30th, 1656, "how forward he was to preach in any of our churches till he was first forbidden by men, and at last disenabled by God. When he could not preach himself as oft and as long as he was able, this learned Gamaliel was not content only but very diligent to sit at the feet of the youngest of his disciples, as diligent an hearer as he had been a preacher. How oft have we seen him walking alone like Jacob of old with his staff to Bethel, the House of God. . . 'He came to his grave in a full age, like as a sheaf of corn cometh in his season.'"

The good Bishop died September 8th, 1656, in the 82nd year of his age, and was buried in the chancel of Heigham Church. From an entry in the Parish Register it would seem that he was buried the same day. The following is a copy of the entry, taken by the kindness of the Rector :—

Sepul. :—Joseph Hall, late Bishoppe of Norwich, was buried September the 8th, 1656."

Blomefield, however, says his remains were interred on the 29th of September, 1656, the day preceding that on which his funeral sermon was preached by Mr. Whitefoot.